EXPLORING PRAYER AND WORSHIP

Written and Edited by Ann Morgan

Contributions by
Anne Jerman, Cristine Curtis
Chelmsford District Beaver Scouts

Illustrated by Ron Branagan

Copyright © 1995
The Scout Association
Baden-Powell House, Queen's Gate, London SW7 5JS

First Edition
Printed in Great Britain by
Wednesday Press Ltd, Southend-on-Sea, Essex
Designed by Spotlight Design Services Ltd

# Contents

	Page
THE BEAVER SCOUT PROGRAMME:	3
INTRODUCTION:	5
GOD LOVES ME - I LOVE GOD:	6
GOD AS A FRIEND:	8
What to pray about	9
Opportunities for prayer and worship	10
Prayers from home	10
Prayers from school	11
Prayers from faith communities	11
SONGS AND HYMNS:	12
MOVING ON:	13
BEAVER SCOUTS LEARN ABOUT THEMSELVES:	14
BEAVER SCOUTS GET TO KNOW PEOPLE:	16
BEAVER SCOUTS EXPLORE:	18
BEAVER SCOUTS CARE:	20
WORSHIP WITH BEAVER SCOUTS:	22
Involve other Beaver Scouts	22
Prayers from faith communities	23
SETTINGS:	24
USEFUL RESOURCES:	27

The Beaver Scout Programme

The Beaver Scout Programme supports and promotes the planning of balanced programmes in the Colony.

It is made up of some areas of activity and a variety of methods which take place within a framework of key principles.

The Beaver Scout Programme is illustrated on the diagram overleaf and is shown as three rings, each of which is equally important.

The **Principles**, shown on the outer ring, underpin all that is done in Beaver Scouting. They describe what Beaver Scouting is all about and ensure that Colonies provide real Scouting for youngsters of Beaver Scout age.

The **Methods**, shown in the middle ring, describe how Beaver Scouts take part in the programme week by week.

The **Activity Areas**, shown in the centre of the diagram, describe what Beaver Scouts do in the programme week by week.

- Beaver Scouts learn about themselves – exploring their feelings and developing good habits of health and personal safety.
- Beaver Scouts get to know people – finding out about people in their family, the family of Scouting, the local community and the wider world.
- Beaver Scouts explore – discovering the exciting world of science, nature and technology, exploring the natural and man-made world.
- Beaver Scouts care – growing in their love of God and responding to the needs of others, the local community and the wider world.

To achieve a balanced programme, Colony Leaders are encouraged to plan at least one activity that fits into each Activity Area, at least once every three or four months. In addition, each of the methods should be used at least once during the same period.

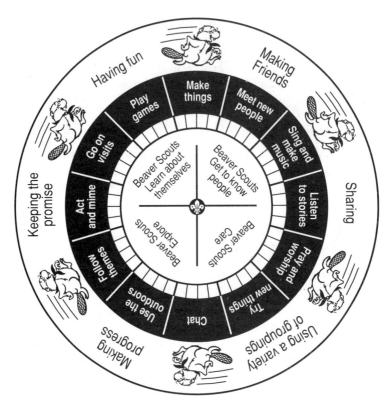

Each Activity Area can be experienced using any of the Methods. Similarly, any of the Methods can be used to introduce any Activity. Thus, the Beaver Scout Programme encourages Leaders to think of different ways to do things as well as different things to do.

Leaders are also encouraged to approach each Activity Area in a variety of ways, by including activities sometimes close to the Beaver Scouts' own experience, sometimes based in the local community and sometimes introducing them to issues in the wider world.

This booklet provides a host of activities in one or more of the Activity Areas and suggests a wide range of ways to do them drawn from the Methods in the Beaver Scout Programme.

Introduction

To discover the need for prayer and worship, on a personal basis and as a shared activity, is one of the five principles of spiritual development agreed jointly by The Scout Association and the major faiths and Christian denominations in the country. The other principles are:

To develop an inner discipline and training.
To be involved in corporate activities.
To understand the natural world around us.
To help create a more tolerant and caring society.

These principles help Leaders to encourage the spiritual development of young people; this is the responsibility of the Association. Each of these principles is equally important. It is recognised that providing opportunities for prayer and worship of God, in an Association that is open to all who accept the principles of the Promise and Law, whatever their religious faith, can seem to be daunting. Hopefully, the contents of this book will dispel this myth and enable you to feel comfortable in encouraging your Beaver Scouts to talk to God as a friend.

Remember, Scouting works in partnership with faith communities to encourage the religious development of young people. It would be helpful to make contact with the local Leaders of the various faiths represented in the Colony to begin to share ideas and methods for achieving this aim. Your Group or District Chaplain will be able to help and support you in this endeavour.

To become Members of the Association, Leaders and young people make a Promise to do their duty to God. The Beaver Scout Promise -

I promise to do my best
to be kind and helpful
and to love God

is worded to be appropriate to the understanding of the six and seven year old. God made us as we are and allowed for differences of size, personality and ability. All religions agree that God wants us to become individuals who can express their love for God and grow into fully enriched people, thus fulfilling our Promise. This is our duty to God.

Colony activities, methods and principles need to incorporate all aspects of the Promise. The booklet *We Promise* gives practical ideas for making this Promise come alive for the Beaver Scouts and, hopefully, will stimulate your own thinking.

God loves me - I love God

Being loved by God and responding to that love is the starting point for Beaver Scouts to grow in their friendship with God. Their level of understanding of God will depend on their family's commitment to a faith and on the religious practices and teaching of their school. Exposure to regular religious teaching may result in a knowledge of God and the ability to communicate with God. Conversely, some of your Beaver Scouts may not have any knowledge of God, of what it means to have a faith or even what is it like to love or be loved. Your own commitment to a faith and an organised community may have a bearing on the approach to helping Beaver Scouts in their understanding of God.

A wall chart of illustrated ideas, based on the following, may help Beaver Scouts to experience and express how:

God loves me . . .
- He gives me the fields, animals and birds to enjoy.
- He gives me friends to play with.
- He gives me my family who love and care for me.
- He gives me my Leaders and other Beaver Scouts to be with.
- He gives me my body to do things.
- He is with me always: when I am happy, when I am lonely, when I am sad.

Examples of their responses could be:

I love God by . . .
- speaking with Him.
- thanking Him.
- taking care of all that He has given me.
- looking after the plants, trees and flowers He has made.
- loving the people He loves.
- looking after God's world by taking rubbish home.

Encourage the Beaver Scouts to add their own ideas.

Dear God, Thank you for all the lovely things on earth and for all the caring people. Thank you for Beavers and all the other lovely creatures. I'll always care for you and be a caring person as long as I live.

Dear God, Make me loving, helpful and kind to all I meet. Amen.

God as a friend

Friends, of any age, develop a mutual trust and respect and need the space and opportunity to share feelings, thoughts and experiences. This can happen quite naturally when Beaver Scouts are engaged in activities which involve co-operation and the opportunity to work in a variety of groupings. Activities and methods used within a Colony programme allow the young people to think for themselves and make choices and decisions that affect their own development. Knowing about the closeness of God and the ability to talk to, and 'share ideas' with, an unseen but real friend should become a normal and accepted part of Colony life.

The language used by most Beaver Scouts is direct, honest and easily understood. What are required are opportunities and occasions to bring your Beaver Scouts closer to God by having real and comfortable conversations.

Invite the Beaver Scouts to draw a picture or write a letter or postcard to God which expresses their feelings about the day's activities. These can then be shared by the Beaver Scouts showing or reading their thoughts or may be displayed as part of a Colony collage.

Dear God, Thank you for all the food in the world. Some more could be useful. Thank you God for being my friend.

Dear God, Help us to be a friend to everyone, to always be kind and helpful even when we don't feel like it. Be with us when we have fun and when we feel sad.

What to pray about

Young people and adults have many reasons to want to pray and worship. These can be praising God for the wonder of everything around us, saying thank you, saying sorry, asking for help and guidance and expressing concern for other people. Each of these categories suggests further areas for prayer. The following illustrates this.

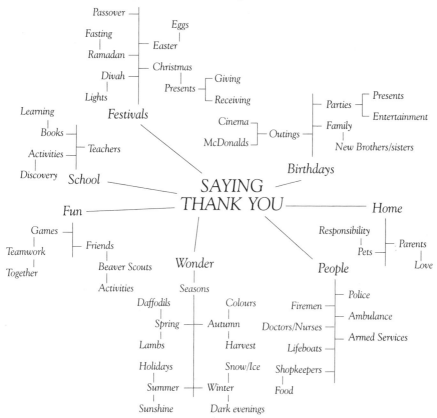

As you can see, the areas about which Beaver Scouts can create their own prayers are numerous and really worthwhile. The following paragraphs look at ways of stimulating ideas so that your Beaver Scouts have fun in being creative, see the task as a natural Colony activity and feel valued for their contribution.

Opportunities for prayer and worship

The recommended Colony programme planning cycle of three to four months provides ample opportunity for a range of topics and types of prayer and worship to be included, both formally and informally.

Let's now explore sources of prayers which are already available and known to the Beaver Scouts and to yourself.

Prayers from home

For some Beaver Scouts it will be quite natural to speak to God within their family. Encourage these Beaver Scouts to share some of the words and atmosphere of these family occasions with their friends in the Colony. Indeed, adult members of a family could be persuaded to spend some time with the Colony to explain their family's style of prayer and worship. The Colony Prayer and Worship book could include a collection of the various traditions found within the faiths represented within the Colony.

Dear God, Help me to be a caring Beaver, to care for my pets, to look after my toys, to tidy my room, to hug my brother when he falls over, to help my Nana with her shopping and to be good to my friends.

Prayers from school

Although Beaver Scouting aims to be different from school, this is an ideal opportunity to take advantage of knowledge and experiences gleaned by young people at school. Some school assemblies and services which celebrate religious and thanksgiving festivals, may involve young people in the planning, writing and reading of prayers. Some will be used on a regular basis and will therefore be familiar. Use these to give confidence to your Beaver Scouts to lead the Colony in prayers. Again, your Colony Prayer and Worship book could include these prayers.

> Dear God, I thank you for my school.
> Please help me to do better every day,
> make me helpful to my teachers and kind
> to my friends.

Prayers from faith communities

It is important to respect the fact that the many faiths encompassed by Scouting place emphasis on different principles and deal with the application of prayer and worship in different ways. Providing the opportunity for your Beaver Scouts to share their own preferred ways of praying with their friends will ensure that these are built into the everyday life of the Colony. Both *The Beaver Scout Leaders' Year Book* and the booklet *Looking at your community* suggest activities to discover a variety of faiths. Information sheets are also available from the Resource Centre at Gilwell Park, Bury Road, Chingford, E4 7QW.

It may be helpful to invite along religious leaders; ensure they can relate to the Beaver Scouts and help them in developing their love of God.

> Dear God, Thank you for the fun we have, thank you
> for the times we share, thank you for our
> Leaders and loving arms that care.

Songs and hymns

Music is another way of communicating with God. Your own experiences and those of your Beaver Scouts will provide a number of songs and music to fit many occasions.

Use the skills and talents of parents, religious leaders and other adults in the Group and District to add their voices to these experiences. Enquire if somebody locally could bring along some handchimes or bells with 'easy to read' music to accompany favourite songs of praise. An electric keyboard or taped music would also provide background music. Your Beaver Scouts could make musical instruments from a variety of items and may even be able to play wind, string or percussion instruments. This is a joyous - and noisy - method of communicating with God.

Hands together softly so,
   D   F G D F D♯ D♯
Little eyes shut tight,
  C D♯ F   C   D
Father just before we go,
   D F G   D F D♯ D♯
Hear our prayers tonight.
    C C   D   C B♭ (lower)
We are all your Beavers here,
  D F G D   F D♯ D♯
This is what we pray,
  C D♯ F   C   D
Keep us safe while dark is near,
  D F G   D   F D♯ D♯
And through every-day.
  C   C   D C B♭
Amen.
 B♭ B♭

Moving on ▶

The previous ideas have tended to suggest the use of existing or well-known words of praise. Undoubtedly, the familiar and tried and tested approaches give comfort and confidence in an area of great diversity.

However, God is the Creator and so is always receptive to creative thinking and used to receiving a variety of messages in different languages.

So how can your Beaver Scouts be encouraged to love, respect and talk to God in a personal and shared way that allows them to express their own thoughts and feelings for a variety of situations?

Using the Activity Areas from the Beaver Scout Programme, the following are some suggested approaches to encouraging prayer in the Colony.

Beaver Scouts learn about themselves

At the age of six and seven years, most Beaver Scouts will have developed the use of senses, feelings and emotions. For example, the use of their hands to touch, hold, create, explore and communicate is worthy of praise.

Make up a few colours of water-based paint in flat trays and let your Beaver Scouts press their hands into the mix. They then place their handprints onto a large piece of paper or cloth. Print out the following poem - or another written by the Beaver Scouts - and fix this below the handprints. The name, date and even a photograph could be added.

> You always clean the fingerprints
> I leave upon the wall.
> I seem to make a mess of things
> Because I am so small.
>
> The years will pass so quickly
> I'll soon be grown like you
> And all my little fingerprints
> Will surely fade from view.
>
> So here's a special handprint
> Of my left and right hand, too
> So you'll recall the very day
> I made this just for you!

Other variations could allow your Beaver Scouts to draw around their own or each others' hands and decorate the shapes. Then list a number of good or not so good things that their hands have been involved in recently. Think about coping without hands and how or what could be used to carry out everyday tasks instead. Following this activity, the Beaver Scouts could say *'Thank you God, with my hands I have ...'* and even *'I am sorry God, with my hands I have ...'*

Use a shoe to focus the Beaver Scouts' attention on thanking God for their feet. Ask the Beaver Scouts where their feet have taken them during the week, what games they have played using feet and how they look after them.

At the end of the evening, all the adults and Beaver Scouts hold hands in a circle and individually say 'Thank you' to God for something good about the day, Colony meeting or personal achievement.

Dear God, Help us to learn words to say kind things, help us to read and write, play games and do maths, and most of all help us to learn to be good.

Beaver Scouts get to know people

At all times in everybody's life, there will be a need to say 'thank you' to God for close family and friends around, in good times and bad. Use occasions that crop up during the Meeting to encourage the Beaver Scouts to create appropriate prayers. After a visit or similar activity, thank God for local services, such as the Police, Fire service, medical teams and the various activity and welfare groups that make up a community.

The concept of a wider community may be difficult for the Beaver Scouts to comprehend because of its remoteness. Pictures of scenes, faces of people and newspaper headlines, all carefully selected, can promote happy and sad emotions and the desire amongst Beaver Scouts to talk about them with God.

Create a special area in your meeting place, perhaps a cosy corner, and have some time put aside to think of God or sing a special song in praise. Set the scene by explaining that some buildings are special places where people go to worship God. These may be churches, mosques and temples and will have various spiritual objects in them. Ask the Beaver Scouts which things they would put in the Colony's special place that are important to them or the Colony. Hopefully this will persuade the Beaver Scouts that, whatever the feelings expressed and the surroundings chosen, it is an acceptable way to talk to God.

Part of Beaver Scouting is about making and developing friendships with family, neighbours and members of the community. The following activity describes how to make friendship sticks which could be given to anyone special who helps or visits the Colony, or for just being a friend.

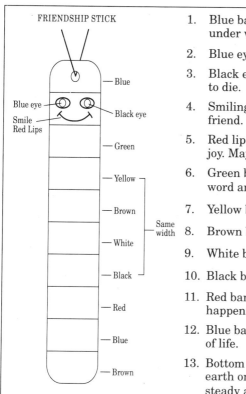

FRIENDSHIP STICK

— Blue

Blue eye
Smile
Red Lips

— Black eye

— Green

— Yellow ⎤
— Brown ⎥ Same
— White ⎥ width
— Black ⎦

— Red

— Blue

— Brown

1. Blue band represents the blue sky under which we all live.

2. Blue eye represents life.

3. Black eye represents death, we all have to die.

4. Smiling face is the trademark of a friend.

5. Red lips, with an upward curve, mean joy. May the smile never be false.

6. Green band is for purity in thought, word and deed. Natural life.

7. Yellow band ⎤ *These bands must be*
8. Brown band *made equal in size, just as man is created equal.*
9. White band *They represent the various races making up*
10. Black band ⎦ *the people of the world.*

11. Red band means hope. Whatever happens, there is always hope.

12. Blue band represents water, the source of life.

13. Bottom brown band is symbolic of the earth on which we tread, standing steady and strong each day.

This is a practical activity which also provides an opportunity for reflection on the sentiments expressed and represented by the different colours. Obviously, the language needs to be appropriate for your Beaver Scouts. They can be encouraged to say 'thank you' to God for these hopes and aspirations by writing prayers or drawing pictures. Ensure that these are used or displayed and included in a Colony prayer and worship book.

Dear God, Help us to play and make friends, to say hello and learn people's names and be a friend to make people happier if they are sad and crying.

Beaver Scouts explore

Whatever a Beaver Scout touches, sees, hears, tastes or smells triggers off a series of what, how and why questions and thoughts. Whether or not a Beaver Scout is able-bodied or has a physical or learning disability, some reaction of wonder will surface. God is responsible for this reaction and will enjoy listening to the expressions of discovery and excitement.

The Beaver Scout programme allows for ample activities and methods to ensure that the young people explore the many aspects of God's world, be they natural or man-made. To turn these into occasions for talking to God, brings to life the wonder of the seasons, the weather, the planets and the characteristics of the environment in which your Beaver Scouts live, whether it be rural, town or inner city. These situations will be a sound basis for establishing a chat line with God. The booklet, *Exploring the environment*, will give you some ideas about activities.

Collect together a range of objects and talk about where they came from. These could be:

- Seeds, plants, flowers, fruits;
- Bread, eggs, cheese, sweets;
- Wood, paper, cardboard, books;
- Wool, cotton, clothes, shoes;
- Tapes, compact discs, telephones, television.

As a practical activity, let the Beaver Scouts taste, arrange or paint pictures of the fruit and flowers (whichever is appropriate); look through the books; use the cardboard, wood and paper for creating a model or shape; feel the textures of the cloth; experiment with sounds, volume and conversation using the audio equipment.

Looking after God's world can involve the Beaver Scouts in making choices and decisions and then taking responsibility for carrying these through. These might involve a campaign for keeping the local environment tidy or studying the pros and cons of recycling materials and considering who can benefit from this process.

These activities, amongst others, will help to keep God's world beautiful and encourage the spontaneous desire to offer thanks.

Being aware of good and not so good incidents during their day, allows the Beaver Scouts to think of words either for thanking God for helping them to be good or saying sorry for a misdemeanour and promising to try to do better tomorrow.

Beaver Scouts care

Listen to any group of Beaver Scouts, or other young people, and you will soon become aware that they have a highly developed sense of caring and concern. Scouting, with its tradition of the good turn, offers young people many practical avenues for expressing this care.

When the Colony has a particular concern or becomes involved in an act of caring, maybe for somebody who is ill or for a community in crisis, you can enlist the extra help that God can give if asked for in prayer. The Colony's work and efforts can be lifted up to God by encouraging Beaver Scouts to tell God what they are doing, why they are doing it and what they hope to achieve. Once again, you are providing an opportunity for building their friendship with God, asking that friend for help and advice and, of course, saying thanks for the successes that will happen.

Make a *caring* and *loving* God chart. Cut out some suitable pictures, such as a religious building, someone praying, a pet, an endangered animal, a fireman and so on. Draw the outlines onto stiff card. Have the Beaver Scouts fit the pictures into the appropriate shapes and perhaps decorate the edge of the card with an attractive border. Encourage the Beaver Scouts to discuss with an adult how the items or activities pictured can help them portray a caring attitude and, therefore, a love of God.

It is nice to know that someone cares. Here is a suggestion to help Beaver Scouts be thoughtful. Giftwrap a small empty box. Tie on a ribbon and attach the following poem or one written by the Beaver Scouts. This gift is not to be unwrapped but should be given to someone special.

> This is a very special gift
> That you can never see,
> The reason it's so special is
> It's just for you, from me.
> Whenever you are lonely,
> Or even feeling blue,
> You only have to hold this gift
> And know I think of you.
> You never can unwrap it,
> Please leave the ribbon tied,
> Just hold the box close to your heart,
> It's filled with love inside.

Dear God, I thank you for people who care for all the animals in the world. Also for people who care for others who are less fortunate than themselves. Thank you for the people who help the young and old people who live on the streets because they have no home of their own. What would the world be like if we had no one who cares? Thank you Lord for these kind people. Amen.

Worship with Beaver Scouts

So far, this booklet has concentrated on ways of speaking or being with God, perhaps in less formal style, seizing the moment for spontaneous prayers and reflection. Here are a few tips and suggestions to help you with those slightly more formal occasions.

'Scouts' Own' is the term used in Scouting to describe an occasion when Scouts come together for a simple form of worship which, whenever possible, they help to lead themselves. A Scouts' Own is not compulsory for young people and some Scouts, because of their faith, may prefer not to attend. However, these occasions are intended to enhance personal and shared spiritual awareness rather than be of a religious nature. Scouts' Own can occur in a variety of places from camps and outdoor environments to Scout Headquarters, school and village halls and places of worship. Members of the Association come together in Colonies, Packs, Troops, Units, Groups, Districts, Areas and Counties and also nationally to worship in this way. The service is often based on the Promise and Law and quite often provides the opportunity to renew the Promise within the Act of Worship.

Worship with Beaver Scouts should reflect the activities, interests and experiences of the young people. When putting together services and deciding on the venue, it is important that the Beaver Scouts can see, can hear and can feel fully involved in the proceedings.

If the worship is being organised by the Group, District or County/Area, make sure that someone on the organising committee understands the needs of Beaver Scouts.

Involve the Beaver Scouts

The principle remains the same as ever, the more you involve the young people, the more successful the event will be. Keep it simple, keep it short, make it practical if possible, and make it sincere. Beaver Scouts will enjoy using their own words to talk to God. Whenever possible, encourage the young people to help plan the event, think of some ideas for prayers and even lead some part of the service if appropriate.

Involve others

Fresh faces are always welcome to attend a Colony Meeting and properly briefed religious leaders are no exception. An invited religious leader should understand the Association's religious policy and how we see our role as one of encouraging young people to make contact with their own faith community. Tactfully remind the religious leader that the audience will be primarily six and seven year olds who need stimulation and involvement. Remind them of the basic rules - keep it simple, short and relevant to the age range.

If the audience includes older Members, it is important that the visiting religious leader is aware of the needs of all the young people being addressed.

Settings

Suggested format for an indoor act of worship before a holiday.

Ask the Beaver Scouts to sit quietly in a circle. Lighting candles and dimming the lights may help create a different atmosphere. Explain that you are all about to thank God for the fun and friendship enjoyed in the Colony during the past few weeks.

Each Lodge places in the circle a collage they have made recording highlights of the recent programmes. One or two Beaver Scouts read a prayer they have written to thank God for Beaver Scouting. The Colony sings a favourite hymn, song or yell - perhaps accompanied on instruments the Beaver Scouts have made.

Close the Meeting with each Beaver Scout and Leader, and any guest, in turn saying 'Goodnight everybody - see you after the holiday.'

Dear God, Thank you for the Beaver Scouts,
Thank you for the fun,
Thank you for the chance to join in as one.
To learn and to play to laugh and to say
'Thank you Lord for the Beaver Scouts',
to guide us in your ways.

Ha Ha Ha, He He He,
A Broomfield Beaver that is me,
With fun and friends together we'll play,
We'll meet again another day.

Suggested format for an act of worship out of doors as part of a Colony visit - perhaps just before lunch.

Choose any appropriate area where the Members of the Colony can gather together in comfort without distractions for five to ten minutes.

Sit the Beaver Scouts in clusters so that they are within comfortable earshot. Ask the Beaver Scouts what they have found most interesting during the morning. Invite any Beaver Scouts that would like to, to show any mementos or gifts they have bought and tell the Colony why they chose them and who they are for. Lead the Colony in a prayer to thank God for the interesting things they have seen and bought so far. Prepare a Beaver Scout to read Grace before the Colony relaxes and eats lunch. A short story appropriate to the setting could be told or read to help calm the Beaver Scouts. The story could be factual, based on information obtained from the local library or tourist information office.

Dear God, May we visit interesting castles, go to the zoo and visit other countries to know your world better. May we visit our Nan and Grandad and enjoy going to town with our Mum. Amen.

Dear God, Thank you for food we eat. Help us share it around the world. Amen.

Suggested format for the end of the evening to celebrate and welcome new Beaver Scouts who have been Invested.

Form the Colony into a circle and ask parents and any visitors to join in as well.

A Beaver Scout reads a prayer asking God to stay with and remain a friend of the new Beaver Scouts at all times. A copy of this prayer could be inserted or written into a card or certificate of welcome, signed by all the Beaver Scouts and adults, and then given to the new Beaver Scouts.

Another option is to give each Beaver Scout or group of Beaver Scouts a balloon. Each Beaver Scout or group writes a wish for the new Member on a slip of paper, which is then inserted into a balloon. The balloons are then inflated and secured. Throw the balloons into the air and let the Beaver Scouts pat them around for a few moments. Eventually, the balloons are caught, burst by the Beaver Scouts and the 'good wish messages' read out. These could be collected and presented to the new Beaver Scout.

Close the Colony Meeting with a tailslap for God.

Dear God, We pray for our new Beaver Scouts enrolled tonight and hope they keep the Promise and enjoy their time at Beaver Scouts.

Dear God, We welcome our new Beaver Scouts and hope they know we are their friends and tell them the Beaver Scout motto 'Fun and Friends'.

Dear God, Please welcome new Beaver Scouts, where they will be kind to each other and love God and have fun. Amen.

Useful resource

An activity pack *God are you still in there?* gives a range of practical ideas to meet the spiritual needs of young people in the Beaver Scout, Cub Scout, Scout and Venture Scout Sections. This pack is available from The Scottish Council, The Scout Association, Fordell Firs, Hillend, Dunfermline, Fife, KY11 5HQ, price £3.50.

Booklets in this series include

Eat without heat

Everyone is special

Five minute fillers

It's a wonderful world

Let's be safe

Let's pretend

Music is fun

We promise

Exploring the environment

Looking at your community

The beaver

Exploring prayer and worship

Fun with science and technology

Notes

Notes

Notes

Notes